Hollywood Classics

CASABLANCA

Hollywood Classics

CASABLANCA

Marie Cahill

SMITHMARK
PUBLISHERS INC.

Published by Smithmark Publishers
112 Madison Avenue
New York, New York 10016

Produced by
Brompton Books Corp.
15 Sherwood Place
Greenwich, CT 06830

ISBN 0-8317-4574-6

Printed in Hong Kong

10 9 8 7 6 5 4 3 2 1

Designed by Ruth DeJauregui

Photo Credits

All photos courtesy of American Graphic Systems
Archives except:
The Paul Ballard Collection, Wagner Library, Rancho
Palos Verdes Art Center 13 (bottom), 24, 33, 38, 73, 78,
90, 100

Page 1: Escorted by Captain Renault, Victor, Ilsa and Rick arrive at the airport, as **Casablanca** races to its dramatic conclusion.
Page 2: Rick (Humphrey Bogart), Ilsa (Ingrid Bergman) and Victor (Paul Henreid) raise their glasses in a toast outside Rick's Café Américain, the focal point of the action.

CASABLANCA

CAST

Rick Blaine	Humphrey Bogart
Ilsa Laszlo	Ingrid Bergman
Victor Laszlo	Paul Henreid
Captain Louis Renault	Claude Rains
Major Strasser	Conrad Veidt
Ugarte	Peter Lorre
Señor Ferrari	Sydney Greenstreet
Sam	Dooley Wilson

Director	Michael Curtiz
Producer	Hal B Wallis
Screenplay	Julius Epstein
	Philip Epstein
	Howard Koch
Director of Photography	Arthur Edeson
Editor	Owen Marks
Score	Max Steiner

From a play by Murray Burnett and Joan Alison

INTRODUCTION

Casablanca could easily have been a 'B' movie featuring Ronald Reagan and Ann Sheridan. Had this been the case, it would have turned up occasionally on the late show, an overly sentimental, mildly entertaining little movie. Fortunately for us, **Casablanca** is one of Hollywood's best films, an unforgettable love story, starring Humphrey Bogart (*right*) and Ingrid Bergman in their most memorable performances.

Set against the backdrop of World War II, **Casablanca** focuses on the romantic torment of Rick Blaine (Bogart), owner of Rick's Café Américain. Unable to forget the past, Rick is cynical and disillusioned, unmoved by the political drama unfolding before him. But Rick wasn't always like this, as the flashback to Paris reveals. The joy that Rick and Ilsa (Bergman) shared in Paris is vividly communicated through Max Steiner's rich score and Arthur Edeson's sumptuous photography. Jilted by the woman he loves, a stunned Rick is left standing in the rain at the train station. Were it not for his loyal friend Sam (Dooley Wilson), who pulls him aboard, he would have missed the last train fleeing Paris before the Nazis occupied the city.

In the hands of a less skillful director and cast, this scenario would have been vapid melodrama. Instead, the film earned three Academy Awards for Best Picture, Best Director and Best Screenplay, as well as a place in the hearts of moviegoers for the last fifty years. According to a survey by *TV Guide*, **Casablanca** is the movie most often repeated on television. In 1983, the British Film Institute polled its members on the 30 best films ever made. Out of the 2000 films nominated, **Casablanca** was number one.

Casablanca was directed by Michael Curtiz. Born Mihaly Kertesz in Budapest, Hungary on 24 December 1892, Curtiz first entered show business as a theatrical extra when he was 14. By the time he was 22, he was directing films. In 1926, after seeing one of Curtiz' films, Jack Warner brought him to America and hired him as a director for Warner Bros, where he quickly established his reputation as a workhorse and a stickler for detail. In 1942, after more than a dozen years in Hollywood, Curtiz finally was awarded an Oscar for Best Director for **Casablanca**.

Like most of Curtiz' films, **Casablanca** is noted for its vivid atmosphere and carefully-crafted performances.

One of the most unforgettable scenes ever to come out of Hollywood is that of Ilsa and Rick, shrouded in fog, as they bid each other farewell at the airport in **Casablanca**. This dramatic conclusion is so perfect that it seems inconceivable that Curtiz could even have considered another ending, but the film featured *two* leading men, and according to the rules of Hollywood the leading man always 'gets the girl.' On one hand, there was Paul Henreid as Ilsa's husband, Victor Laszlo, the brave Czech resistance fighter. Certainly such a noble character deserved to win Ilsa. Moreover, Henreid believed his credentials as an actor entitled him to win the heart of the leading lady. Henreid had just completed **Now, Voyager**, with the famous scene in which he held two cigarettes in his lips, lit them and passed one to Bette Davis. Clearly, he was firmly established as a romantic lead.

On the other side was Humphrey Bogart. Though he was not the typical handsome leading man, with his performance a year earlier in **The Maltese Falcon** Bogart had shown that he was more than capable of playing a romantic lead. As Sam Spade in **The Maltese Falcon**, Bogart finally moved beyond the stock roles to which Warners had relegated him. **Casablanca** smoothed out the remaining rough edges and refined the Bogey screen persona—the world-wise and weary tough guy who plays by his own set of rules. Underneath the seemingly impenetrable surface he is susceptible to a vulnerable romanticism.

Rick could have come across as an unbelievable character. Supposedly a tough guy, he was a man so torn apart by a love gone wrong that he refused to allow a once-favorite song to be played in his café. Later in the film, when Ilsa confronts him with a gun, he tells her 'Go ahead and shoot. You'd be doing me a favor.' The lines border on the lachrymose, but Bogart played the role as only Bogart could. Off screen Bogart reportedly worried about whether the audience would believe that a woman of Ingrid Bergman's beauty would love such an atypical leading man. On screen, when Ingrid Bergman as Ilsa looked at Rick, all doubts were laid to rest.

Ingrid Bergman came to Hollywood in 1939 to star in David O Selznick's **Intermezzo**. A woman of transcendent beauty, she exuded radiance, strength and vitality in all her

Right, above and below: Making a movie isn't all work. After hours, the cast and crew get together for some fun and relaxation. In the photo *at top*, an amused Michael Curtiz looks on as Bogart and Bergman share a dance.

films. Though not the first choice for the part of Ilsa Laszlo, no other actress would have equalled the performance given by the incomparable Ingrid Bergman (*left*). Throughout the filming of **Casablanca**, Bergman was constantly asking Curtiz which man she would finally choose. She decided to play it down the middle, and the end result is that we see a woman torn by uncertainty. From the first moment she appeared on the screen, she played the part with a grace and indecisiveness that heightened the tension of the final airport scene. Does she choose romance, passion, the carefree life that she and Rick shared in Paris, or does she stand by her husband's side, the loyal, inspiring wife? In the end, she does not have to choose at all. 'I don't know what's right any longer. You have to think for both of us, for all of us' she tells Rick. And he does, sending her off with her husband, while he and Louis Renault take on the Nazis.

Casablanca is one of those rare movies in which all the pieces fit together beautifully. The script, though incomplete until the final hour, is witty and tense. Written by Howard Koch and Julius and Philip Epstein, the script won an Academy Award for Best Screenplay. The music is equally superb. Max Steiner's score evokes the appropriate mood, but to film lovers everywhere, it is the song *As Time Goes By* that makes the movie. Performed by Dooley Wilson, who gave a solid performance as Rick's piano-playing friend, the song is responsible for the movie's oft-quoted line 'Play it again, Sam.' In reality, Bogey never uttered those immortal words. What he really said was, 'Play it, Sam. You played it for her. Now play it for me.'

Along with Dooley Wilson, the rest of the supporting cast contributed almost flawless performances. The duo of Sydney Greenstreet and Peter Lorre, who were unforgettable in *The Maltese Falcon*, made a reprise performance, this time with Lorre playing the sly Ugarte and Greenstreet as Señor Ferrari, the owner of the Blue Parrot café. SZ Sakall, another Warner Brothers contract player and, like Curtiz and Lorre, a native Hungarian, brought charm to the part of Carl, the head waiter. Claude Rains as Captain Louis Renault, the Prefect of Police, is both humorous ('I'm only a poor corrupt official') and menacing. In the end, he is a hero. When Rick shoots Major Strasser, Louis tells the police to 'Round up the usual subjects.' The camera fades as Rick and Louis walk off together, united in purpose, and the movie concludes with one of the finest closing lines ever written—'Louis, I think this is the start of a beautiful friendship.'

CASABLANCA

Right, above: In this early scene, Major Strasser is met by Captain Renault, the Prefect of Police in Casablanca, who welcomes him on behalf of unoccupied France. Renault claims to be politically neutral, saying he blows with the prevailing wind and 'the prevailing wind is from Vichy,' the new government of unoccupied France that collaborated with the Nazis.

Major Strasser's immediate concern is to find the man who has killed two German couriers for the letters of transit they were carrying. Signed by General de Gaulle, the letters represent freedom. Strasser fears that the letters will fall into the hands of Victor Laszlo, a hero of the resistance movement.

Right, below: The filming of the scene in which Major Heinrich Strasser arrives in Casablanca. Unlike most movies, **Casablanca** was filmed sequentially, and for good reason: The script wasn't finished when filming began. In spite of this apparent difficulty, the plot progresses at a quick pace, neatly weaving all the tangled story threads to a poignant conclusion.

Though Rick's Café Américain seems to provide a lull from the storm, beneath the gaiety lies a tinderbox ready to ignite. In the scene *at left*, a suspicious Nazi keeps his eye on Carl (SZ Sakall), the maître d', as Sascha (Leonid Kinskey), the Russian bartender, looks on.

Leonid Kinskey was born on 18 April 1902 in St Petersburg, Russia. After leaving Russia he toured the theaters of Europe and South America before settling in Hollywood in the early 1930s. He played light supporting parts, typically those of a caricatured foreigner. Kinskey retired from film in the late 1940s, returning briefly in the mid-1950s before turning to television as both an actor and a director-producer.

Kinskey's films include **Trouble in Paradise** (1932), **Duck Soup** (1933), **Les Misérables** (1935), **The General Died at Dawn** (1937), **The Story of Vernon and Irene Castle** (1939), **I Married an Angel** (1943) and **The Man With the Golden Arm** (1955).

Like the character he played in **Casablanca**, SZ Sakall was forced to flee his homeland to escape persecution by the Nazis. Born Eugene Gero Sakall in Budapest, Hungary on 2 February 1884, Sakall was known for his comedic skills on the Central European stage and screen, under the stage name of Szöke Sakall. A popular star in early German musicals, he was often cast in musicals and comedies. Sakall arrived in Hollywood after the outbreak of World War II and soon won the hearts of American audiences. Affectionately known as 'Cuddles,' Sakall's trademarks were his fractured English, flabby jowls and excitable personality.

After **Casablanca**, Sakall appeared in numerous movies, including **The Human Comedy** (1943), **Christmas in Connecticut** (1945), **Romance on the High Seas** (1948), **In the Good Old Summertime** (1949), and **Lullaby of Broadway** (1951).

The first glimpse we have of Rick is of his hand as he signs his 'OK.' As the camera zooms in, we see him sitting alone, a chess board before him. The audience has learned about him from the other characters, but what has been gleaned is that Rick is a man of mystery.

Rick is soon joined by Ugarte, played by Peter Lorre. 'You despise me, don't you?' he asks Rick.

'If I gave it any thought, I probably would,' was Rick's cynical reply.

In this pivotal scene (*left*), Ugarte requests a favor from Rick. Ugarte has killed the German couriers for the valuable letters of transit, which he plans to sell 'for more money than you can imagine.' He wants Rick to safeguard the stolen letters for a few hours until he can sell them.

A former bank clerk, Lorre received his stage training in Vienna. After acting for several years in Austria, Switzerland and Germany, he rose to international fame with his performance in **M**, Fritz Lang's 1931 masterpiece about a psychopathic child murderer. Lorre's sinister yet pathetic expression gave the character a frightening realism.

Once in the United States, Lorre promptly landed superb roles in two films: as a love-crazed surgeon in Karl Freund's **Mad Love** (1935) and as Raskolnikov in Josef von Sternberg's **Crime and Punishment** (1935). He went on to play both leading and supporting roles in numerous films, often appearing as the mysterious and menacing foreigner. Some of his most notable roles were in Warner Bros dramas. In addition to **Casablanca**, Lorre appeared in **The Maltese Falcon** (1941), **The Mask of Dimitrios** (1944), **Three Strangers** (1946) and **The Verdict** (1946).

Lorre temporarily returned to Germany in 1951 to write, star in and direct **Der Verlorene/The Lost One**, a remarkable film done in the style of the German expressionism of the 1920s. He died in 1964 of a heart seizure.

Rick's Café Américain provides a focal point for the movie. As Renault tells Major Strasser: 'Everyone comes to Rick's.' And indeed they do. Rick's is a microcosm of the world, peopled with a variety of nationalities and ideologies. Refugees from war-torn Europe find their way to Rick's, hoping to secure an exit visa. The lucky ones then scurry to Lisbon and eventually to freedom in America. Meanwhile, Nazis sip champagne and mingle with citizens from countries whose governments the Third Reich has overthrown.

Left: Rick casually hides the letters of transit given to him by Ugarte at Sam's piano, while Sam (Dooley Wilson) treats the crowd to a rousing version of 'Knock on Wood.'

Dooley Wilson began his career as a minstrel performer when he was 12. He tried his hand at vaudeville and acted in stock, and in the 1920s was a singing drummer with his own band in Paris and London. After his stint abroad, he starred in Federal Theater productions and a Broadway musical before his screen debut in 1942. Even though most of Wilson's roles were minor supporting parts, he has a earned a place in film history for the bit part of Sam the piano player. Rumor has it, however, that Wilson didn't know how to play the piano and his playing was dubbed.

Humphrey Bogart was nominated for an Academy Award for Best Actor for his performance as Rick Blaine, the owner of Rick's Café Américain. Though the award went to Paul Lukas for **Watch on the Rhine**, Bogey's performance has stood the test of time.

Above: Sydney Greenstreet brought a touch of urbanity to the role of Señor Ferrari, the owner of the Blue Parrot café. Knowing Sam's popularity, Ferrari would like to try to persuade Sam to work for him.

Right: Greenstreet had originally intended to make his fortune as a tea planter in Ceylon, but a drought forced him to revise his plans. He returned to England, where he managed a brewery and held various other jobs until he enrolled in acting school. In 1902, Greenstreet made his London stage debut as a murderer in *Sherlock Holmes*, and two years later debuted on Broadway in *Everyman*. He appeared in numerous productions in New York and on the road, playing a wide range of roles, from Shakespeare to musical comedy.

In 1941, Greenstreet, then 61, made his screen debut, giving a fabulous performance as the ruthless Kasper Gutman in **The Maltese Falcon**. He remained in Hollywood, appearing in a number of Warner Bros melodramas, earning a following as large as his own girth.

Overleaf: As the owner of the Blue Parrot, Casablanca's other popular and prosperous night spot, Ferrari would like to double his wealth by buying out Rick. Rick tells him, 'It's not for sale at any price,' but the events of the evening will cause him to reconsider Ferrari's offer.

Left: 'What a fool I was to fall for a man like you.' Depressed by her ill-fated romance with Rick, Yvonne (Madeleine LeBeau), a French refugee, attempts to drown her sorrow at the bar, whereupon Rick promptly sends her home in a cab.

At this point, the audience knows very little about Rick's past. His earlier discussion with Ferrari has revealed that he is an isolationist, and it would appear that he is a loner in matters of the heart as well.

The aura of mystery surrounding Rick continues to build, as Rick steps outside to join Renault (*overleaf*), who speculates about Rick's reasons for leaving America: 'Did you abscond with the church funds? I'd like to think you killed a man. It's the romantic in me.'

When Renault asks him why he came to Casablanca, Rick responds with a suitably wry remark:

'I came to Casablanca for the waters.'
'What waters? We're in the middle of a desert.'
'I was misinformed.'

After exchanging witticisms, Renault gets to the point, informing Rick that Victor Laszlo is on his way to Casablanca and will certainly appear at Rick's, where exit visas are frequently bought and sold. Renault warns Rick not to assist Laszlo. Though Rick maintains the image of neutrality, it wasn't always so. He was a gun-runner for Ethiopia in its losing fight against the takeover by fascist Italy, and he fought for the Loyalists in the Spanish Civil War. As Renault astutely points out, Rick has a history of aiding the underdog. Rick, however, insists that he has no interest in helping Laszlo, and asserting that the underground leader is quite capable of escaping on his own, he bets Renault 10,000 francs on Laszlo's ingenuity. Rick would have preferred to bet 20,000 francs, but Renault explains, 'I'm just a poor corrupt official.'

Left: As Captain Louis Renault, Claude Rains played the sort of role at which he excelled: the suave and charming villain. Rains made his debut on the London stage at the age of 11, but didn't turn to the silver screen until he was middle-aged. By that time, he was a highly regarded stage performer, known for his expressive face, which, ironically, was bandaged or hidden from view for his first Hollywood role in **The Invisible Man** (1933).

Whether playing the lead or a supporting part, Rains' distinctive voice and polished manner enhanced a wide range of films. He was nominated for an Academy Award for **Casablanca**, as well as for **Mr Smith Goes to Washington** (1939), **Mr Skeffington** (1944) and **Notorious** (1946), but Oscar eluded him.

Above: Because 'Everyone comes to Rick's,' Captain Renault naturally brings Major Strasser there his first night in Casablanca. Renault's remark is an allusion to the play on which the movie is based, *Everybody Comes to Rick's* by Murray Burnett and Joan Alison.

Right: Major Strasser (left) and Captain Renault (right) have convened at Rick's Café Américain to await the arrest of Ugarte. As the top official in Casablanca, Renault wants to look good in Strasser's eyes and has posted two guards at every door so that Ugarte has no chance for escape. An elegant repast of caviar and fine French champagne provides a striking contrast to the scene that is about to played out before their eyes.

A distinguished German character actor, Conrad Veidt began his career at the Deutsches Theater in Berlin in 1913. He achieved a level of prominence in German expressionist films, often as a demented and tortured character, such as Cesare in **The Cabinet of Dr Caligari** (1919). His performance in the title role of **The Student of Prague** (1926), as well as a number of other literary and historical roles, earned him worldwide praise and took him to Hollywood. Veidt returned to Germany with the advent of sound, but immigrated to England with his Jewish wife when the Nazis came to power. Later, while visiting Germany, the Nazis tried to detain him, creating an international sensation and forcing a dramatic rescue by his employers, Gaumont British. In 1940 Veidt journeyed to Hollywood, where he found himself playing the very type of villains who had haunted his own life—Nazi officers. His career was cut short by a fatal heart attack in 1943.

31

Above: Ugarte is arrested at the roulette table. As he cashes in his winnings, he tries to flee. But the net closes in on him, and there is nowhere to hide (*right*). Though the arrest is handled by the local authorities, Renault is collaborating with the Nazis. This is one of the few scenes in which World War II comes to the forefront. For the most part, director Michael Curtiz decided to focus on the romantic aspects of the story, using World War II as a backdrop and ignoring its brutal realities.

Though the film whitewashes Nazism, the Nazis nonetheless objected to the film, considering it anti-Nazi propaganda. **Casablanca** was banned in Germany until after the war, and when it was finally shown, the censors had deleted 20 minutes of footage, including all references to Nazis and all of Conrad Veidt's scenes.

Left: Ugarte runs to Rick, whining for help, but Rick 'sticks his neck out for nobody.' When the Nazis discover Ugarte does not have the valuable letters of transit, he is of no use to them and is killed.

The tough guy image is central to the cult legend that surrounds Humphrey Bogart, and to a certain extent the image has its roots in the man himself. Dave Chase, a Hollywood restauranteur once remarked, 'Bogart's a helluva nice guy till 11:30 pm. After that he thinks he's Bogart.' Even as a young man Bogart was known for his hard-headedness. Kicked out of prep school for disciplinary problems, Bogart never made it to Yale, where his surgeon father had planned for him to study medicine. Instead, Bogart joined the navy when the United States entered World War I. While on duty on the USS *Leviathan*, Bogart was injured during a shelling and left with a partially paralyzed upper lip—the source of his characteristic tight-set mouth and lisp.

After **Casablanca**, Bogart successfully reprised his tough guy image in various films, such as **To Have and Have Not** (1945), **The Big Sleep** (1946) and **Key Largo** (1948). His co-star in these three films was Lauren Bacall, who became his fourth and final wife.

In the 1950s, Bogart demonstrated the range of his skill with widely diverse roles in such films as **The Caine Mutiny** (1954), **Sabrina** (1954), **The Barefoot Contessa** (1954), and **The African Queen** (1952), for which he received his one and only Academy Award.

Ingrid Bergman (*right*) makes her entrance in **Casablanca** in the seventy-fifth shot–relatively late in the film for a central character. Renault has spoken of her beauty, but we know nothing else of her.

When she does finally appear, both Ilsa and her husband, the heroic Victor Laszlo, are dressed in white, symbolizing their good and noble cause.

At the first opportunity, Ilsa speaks to Sam and asks him to play *As Time Goes By*–'Play it once, Sam. For old time's sake. Play it, Sam. Play *As Time Goes By*.' Reluctantly, Sam complies.

When Rick hears the old, familiar melody–which he has asked Sam not to play–he angrily rushes over to the piano and sees Ilsa. He joins her and Victor at their table (*overleaf*), for a drink, causing Renault to remark 'A precedent has been broken.' Rick *never* drinks with his customers. Renault and Victor Laszlo, as well as the audience, immediately sense the chemistry between Ilsa and Rick. Feigning an air of indifference, Ilsa acts as if she only vaguely recalls the last time they met. Rick, however, remembers every detail: 'The Germans wore grey; you wore blue.'

Since Ilsa left him, Rick has maintained an image of cynical aloofness, but with her reappearance he succumbs to his despair. This scene (*right*) is notable for a number of famous lines. As a drunken and depressed Rick waits for Ilsa to return, he mumbles to himself 'Of all the gin joints in all the towns in all the world she walks into mine.'

Of course, this scene is also is famous for the line most often identified with the film, 'Play it again, Sam.' In reality that line was never uttered. What Rick really said to Sam was 'You played it for her. You can play it for me. If she can stand it, I can. Play it.'

Right: As Sam plays *As Time Goes By*, the scene dissolves into a flashback of Rick and Ilsa, in love in Paris. For the moment they are happy and carefree. We see them merrily driving through the French countryside, smiling gaily. Their happiness will be all too brief, for Ilsa will soon disappear from Rick's life and the Germans will occupy the city.

The flashback is a useful narrative technique that has been employed successfully in a number of well-known films. As in **Casablanca**, a flashback can be used to explain an event that occurred before the main story began. Flashbacks may also be used to clarify an element of the plot, such as the scene of the crime in a mystery, or to provide keys to a character's motivation, as in **Death of a Salesman** (1952). A flashback can be of any length, from several frames representing a memory, such as Rick's recollection of his days in Paris with Ilsa, to almost the entire film, as in **Citizen Kane** (1941) and **Rashomon** (1951). In these two films, the flashback technique also allows several characters to tell their versions of the same event.

Flashbacks figured prominently in two other Bogart films. In **Dead Reckoning** (1947), the entire plot unfolds in a flashback as Bogart's character confesses to a priest. **The Barefoot Contessa** (1954) used the ultimate flashback technique—the flashback within a flashback, in which Bogart, while attending Ava Gardner's funeral (the present) recalls the night she visited him in his hotel room (flashback) to tell him about her wedding (flashback within a flashback).

As Ilsa, Ingrid Bergman exemplifies decency and vulnerability, an image that would recur in many of her subsequent films. She played a nun stricken with tuberculosis in **The Bells of St Mary's** (1945) and was even elevated to sainthood with her performance in **Joan of Arc** (1948).

Ilsa's image of goodness is a credit to Bergman's skill. From the moment she appears on screen, the audience accepts her and sympathizes with her character. Bergman makes the audience ignore the harsh realities. Though she radiates goodness, Ilsa's life is filled with moral ambiguity. Through the flashback, the audience learns that she had a passionate romance with Rick shortly after the presumed death of her husband. Later, she agrees to run away with Rick.

After reviewing the script, a reader for Warner Bros pointed out that Ilsa and Rick's relationship 'is one that does not seem permissible in a film.' Perhaps on paper, but on screen all moral ambiguity is forgotten.

Left: While in Paris, Rick and Ilsa live for the moment. She is guarded about her past, and Rick, for the most part, doesn't press her. When he does start to question her, she reminds him of their promise to ask no questions, and they celebrate their happiness with a toast: 'Here's looking at you, kid.'

The joyful mood of Ilsa and Rick's time together in Paris is effectively captured by the sumptuous camera work of Arthur Edeson, who was nominated for an Academy Award for Best Cinematography for **Casablanca**.

Edeson began his career as a portrait photographer, switching to film during the era of silent films, first as a camera operator and then advancing to director of photography. With the advent of sound, Edeson was instrumental in developing location sound photography for his work on the Western **In Old Arizona**. Recognized as a master at creating atmosphere, Edeson had a long and fruitful career with Warner Bros. His credits include **The Three Musketeers** (1921), **The Thief of Bagdad** (1924), **Stella Dallas** (1925), **All Quiet on the Western Front** (1930), **Frankenstein** (1931), **Mutiny on the Bounty** (1935), **Gold Diggers of 1937** (1936), **The Mask of Dimitrios** (1944), **Three Strangers** (1946) and **My Wild Irish Rose** (1947).

Sam is an integral part of the days in Paris. In the photograph *at right*, Humphrey Bogart and Dooley Wilson exchange pleasantries on the set. Their camaraderie off stage is a reflection of their screen relationship. The role is notable because Sam, a black man, is portrayed as Rick's friend and equal at a time when Hollywood largely restricted black actors to playing cabbies and porters.

In addition to **Casablanca**, Dooley Wilson appeared in **My Favorite Blonde** (1942), **Stormy Weather** (1943), **Seven Days Ashore** (1944), **Racing Luck** (1948), **Come to the Stable** (1949) and **Passage West** (1951). He died in 1953.

Right: Rick and Ilsa worriedly scan the papers for news of the war, their concern reflected in their faces.

Throughout the flashback sequence, we hear Max Steiner's score. The music for **Casablanca** was typical Steiner — melodious and rich, and closely associated with the visual images.

A musical prodigy, Maximilian Steiner was born on 10 May 1888 in Vienna. At the age of 13, he graduated from Vienna's Imperial Academy of Music, after completing the eight-year course in just a year's time. The next year he wrote the book and lyrics and composed the score for a musical that ran two years on the Vienna stage. By the time he was 16, Steiner was a professional conductor.

Steiner emmigrated to the United States in 1914, ending up on Broadway as a conductor and orchestrator for the musicals of George White, Florenz Ziegfield and Victor Herbert. He left for Hollywood in 1929 when filmmakers discovered sound. Film had long used music to change the mood or enhance the atmosphere, but under the influence of Steiner, among others, the emphasis shifted toward making the score an integral part of the film.

Steiner's scores earned him 19 nominations for Academy Awards, including one for **Casablanca**. He won three times — for **The Informer** (1935), **Now, Voyager** (1942) and **Since You Went Away** (1944). In all, Steiner scored more than 200 films, but he is probably best known for the score of **Gone With the Wind** (1939), one of the longest and richest scores in film history.

Left: At La Belle Aurore. Sam plays *As Time Goes By*, while Paris waits for the Germans to descend on the city. The owner of the café has announced that he will water his garden with champagne before he lets the Nazis drink it. Rick is willing to help him dispose of the champagne, but Ilsa cannot ignore what is happening. Her look of distress is more than her fear of the German occupation. She has just learned that her husband, Victor Laszlo, is alive and waiting for her outside Paris.

Right: Though they know very little about each other, Ilsa knows enough about Rick's past to know that the Germans will look for him. Ilsa tells him he must leave Paris at once.

Casablanca will be remembered as one of the great love stories of all time, and like many of the silver screen's great romances, Ilsa and Rick's love is something greater than themselves. Like Heathcliff and Cathy in **Wuthering Heights** (1939) or Rhett Butler and Scarlett O'Hara in **Gone With the Wind** (1939), Ilsa and Rick belong to the tradition of ill-fated romances, of lovers torn apart by forces beyond their control.

Having convinced audiences, as well as himself, that he could play a romantic lead, Humphrey Bogart went on to star with some of Hollywood's most alluring leading ladies, but his best romantic roles would be in the films that found him opposite his own wife, Lauren Bacall. They met and fell in love on the set of **To Have and Have Not** (1943) and were soon married. Though they seemed an impropable pair — she was only 18 when they met, he was 44 — the marriage, unlike Bogart's three previous ones, was a happy one that endured until Bogart's death from throat cancer in 1957.

Right: Quintessential Bogart, in trench coat and fedora. As Rick Blaine, Bogart gave his finest good guy-bad guy performance.

Bogart's performance in **Casablanca** guaranteed him a place in annals of film history, but it was an honor that came after a long apprenticeship. Bogart's acting career began in a round-about way after his discharge from the navy following World War I. With the help of a family friend, he found a job in the theater as an office boy and worked his way up to road company manager and stage manager. After hanging around backstage he was bit by the acting bug, but the New York theater world was less than enthusiastic about his abilities. In the oft-quoted review of the play *Swiftly* (1922), critic Alexander Woollcott referred to Bogart's acting as 'what is usually and mercifully described as inadequate.' Bogart, however, was not deterred and went on to play numerous, albeit indifferent, stage roles throughout the 1920s.

Bogart eventually turned his sights to Hollywood, but roles were no better there, and he found himself scuttling back and forth between coasts, searching for the right part. His luck finally changed in 1935, when he landed the part of the gangster Duke Mantee in the Broadway production of Robert E Sherwood's *The Petrified Forest.* Warner Bros acquired the film rights to the play, intending to cast Edward G Robinson in the Bogart part, but Leslie Howard, who had played the leading role on Broadway, threatened to quit unless the part of Duke Mantee went to Bogey. Warners acceded to Howard's demands, **The Petrified Forest** (1936) was a great success, and Humphrey Bogart was finally on the path to stardom.

The path, however, was somewhat rocky. Between 1936 and 1940, Bogart appeared in 28 films, usually playing a gangster. The turning point came in 1941 with **High Sierra**. Though cast again as a villain, Bogart's part—with thanks to screenwriter John Huston—was a step above the others. Later in the year, when Huston was given the opportunity to direct his first film, he found himself working once again with Bogart as Sam Spade in **The Maltese Falcon**. The role had been offered to George Raft, but he turned it down, probably because he didn't want to work with an inexperienced director. Raft's loss was Bogart's gain, for Sam Spade was the best role Bogart had had the opportunity to play. It proved that Bogart could play the hero and romantic lead—and thus was born the Bogey legend.

Right: Rick has agreed to flee the city, but only if Ilsa comes with him. In spite of the turmoil surrounding them, he is feeling happy and lighthearted and tries to joke with her about getting married on the train. Ilsa, however, is distraught. Her sense of duty has compelled her to go to her husband. Knowing that Rick will not leave Paris without her, she makes plans to meet him at the train station, though she has no intention of meeting him there. She wants to tell him the truth, but she cannot. Instead she tells him, 'Kiss me as if it were the last time.'

Overleaf: Rick arrives at the train station at the appointed hour only to discover that Ilsa is not there. He sends Sam to her hotel and he returns with a letter from Ilsa that reads 'I cannot go with you or ever see you again. You must not ask why. Just believe that I love you. Go, my darling, and God bless.'

 The camera zooms in on the letter, as the words are washed away in the rain. Stunned by the news that the woman he loves is gone from his life forever, he can only stand in the rain, barely comprehending what has happened.

Above: Humphrey Bogart and Ingrid Bergman discuss the nuances of Ilsa and Rick's relationship with director Michael Curtiz.

Right: The flashback sequence ends, and now the audience knows more about the situation than Rick himself. Ilsa returns to the café to see Rick. She tries to explain why she left him in Paris, telling him a story about a girl who came to Paris and met a 'very great and courageous man...who opened for her a whole beautiful world full of knowledge and thoughts and ideals. Everything she ever knew or became was because of him and she looked up to him and worshipped him, with a feeling that she supposed was love.'

Rick is in no mood for explanations. His manner is insulting, and Ilsa walks out *without* telling him that she was married to Laszlo while they were together in Paris.

Left: Bogart was worried about playing the romantic lead opposite a woman as beautiful as Ingrid Bergman. Though he had starred in roughly 40 movies, it wasn't until **The Maltese Falcon** the year before **Casablanca** that he had played a romantic lead. He wondered whether audiences would believe that Bergman could fall in love with an ordinary-looking guy. Later, he said of his performance, 'I didn't do anything I've never done before. But when the camera moves in on that Bergman face, and she's saying she loves you, it would make anybody look romantic.'

Bogart also had his doubts about the script. Bogey played tough guys, not a wimp who had been left broken-hearted by a love affair. Producer Hal Wallis agreed to strengthen the part, as he would also do for Paul Henreid. On the advice of his acting coach, Bogart used a subtle technique to strengthen his character. He stood still and made Ilsa come to him. The end result is a character left disillusioned by a love affair gone wrong. Rick is worldly and cynical, but certainly not weak.

Above: A pensive Rick looks on as Sam, his alter ego, entertains the crowd at Rick's Café Américain.

Right: The morning after Ugarte's arrest, Major Strasser meets with Captain Renault. Strasser rightly assumes that Ugarte gave the letters of transit to Rick.

Though the film ignores the brutalities of Nazism, there is a brief moment of realism when we learn that Ugarte has been killed. Without the letters of transit, he is worthless to his captors.

Although he is a Frenchman, Captain Louis Renault was considered a Nazi collaborator because he was a representative of the Vichy government, which was created when France surrendered to Germany in 1940.

Torn by internal strife and still weakened from the First World War, France was in no position for another war, but when Hitler invaded Poland in September 1939, France, along with England, declared war against Germany.

Less than a year later, France was on the verge of collapse. On 11 June 1940, the government retreated from Paris, which was declared an 'open city' to spare it from destruction by the Nazis. As the Nazis advanced through central France, almost without opposition, the French government under the newly-elected Marshal Henri Pétain, the 84-year-old hero of World War I, voted in favor of an armistice.

On 22 June 1940, France signed the terms of surrender. Though the countryside had emerged relatively unscathed from the brief fighting, roughly 1,500,000 men had been taken as prisoners of war and the nation, as a whole, was demoralized by the country's brutal defeat.

Germany occupied the northern half and the western coast of France, allowing unoccupied France, the 'Free Zone,' to operate as a puppet government at Vichy. Marshal Pétain, as head of the Vichy government, declared an end to the democratic French parliament and made himself dictator on 11 July 1940. France was now divided physically and philosophically, as illustrated by the characters in **Casablanca**.

On one hand, there were those, such as Louis Renault, who chose to support Pétain and therefore Hitler. On the other hand were the French patriots—the 'Free French' (later Fighting French) forces in England who had reunited under the leadership of General Charles de Gaulle. Though the Vichy government considered the Free French forces to be traitors, the Free French had the support of the people at home and abroad.

Casablanca is peppered with people of various nationalities—Victor Laszlo for one—who subscribe to the Free French ideals, and when **Casablanca** concludes, Renault has undergone a change of heart, and he and Rick join the Free French.

Right: Strasser orders Renault to search Rick's Café Améri-cain for the missing letters of transit. Confident that Rick is just another blundering American, Strasser is sure the papers will easily be found. 'You mustn't underestimate American blundering,' Renault remarks. 'I was with them when they blundered into Berlin in 1918.'

The Americans would soon be blundering into French North Africa. On 8 November 1942, American forces under Lieutenant General Dwight D Eisenhower landed at Casablanca and other points on the Mediterranean and Atlantic coasts, capturing strategic points in Algeria and Morocco.

Germany reacted by occupying the rest of France, an action which spurred thousands of Frenchmen to form an underground organization known as *Le Maquis* (the under-brush). This force later became the FFI, or French Forces of the Interior, and would join de Gaulle's army when the Allies landed at Normandy on 6 June 1944.

Meanwhile, as most of the world was being torn apart by war, Hollywood was still making movies, and as Eisenhower and his troops were landing in Casablanca, **Casablanca** the movie was released to limited theaters in the United States. Two months later, in January 1943, as Franklin Delano Roosevelt and Winston Churchill met in Casablanca for the historic 'unconditional surrender' con-ference, the movie was released across the country, and the word 'Casablanca,' whether referring to the war or to the movie, was on everyone's lips.

CADIZ
GIBRALTAR
TANGER
CEUTA
RIF
RABAT
FÈS
CASABLANÇA
MAROC
MOGADOR
MARRAKECH
ERFOUD

Above: At the appointed hour, Victor and Ilsa arrive at Captain Renault's office to discuss obtaining exit visas. Renault, of course, has no interest in helping them.

Above: Major Strasser guarantees Ilsa and Victor safe passage to Lisbon *if* Laszlo will give them the names of the resistance leaders throughout Europe. Laszlo, of course, refuses. 'If I didn't give them to you in a concentration camp, where you had more persuasive methods at your disposal, I certainly won't give them to you now.'

Left: Rick stops by the Blue Parrot, Ferrari's night club. Filled with representatives from numerous European nations dressed in their finest evening wear, Rick's has a very Continental flavor. The Blue Parrot, on the other hand, is frequented by the native population, and, with its belly dancers and strange music, is—to the Western eye—quite exotic.

The atmosphere of the Blue Parrot typified that of Casablanca itself, for it was a city of diverse cultures, an Arab nation influenced by its French rulers. Morocco had been under French control since early in the twentieth century, and under the French, the city of Casablanca had been transformed from an insignificant Arab town into a glistening city and a major port of North Africa. The French introduced modern agricultural methods, developed mines and built highways, but they left the ancient Moorish buildings and, to a certain extent, its way of life intact. Thus, the mixing of the old and the new, the French and the Arab was very much a part of the city's character, and it made Casablanca a strange and wondrous place.

Left: Ferrari feigns concern over the death of Ugarte, but Rick sees right through him, calling him a 'fat hypocrite.' Ferrari understands Rick just as well as Rick understands him. A black market racketeer, Ferrari is anxious to put his hands on the stolen papers, and, like Strasser and Renault, he is sure that Rick is the key to the missing papers.

Sydney Greenstreet was one of the finest villains to grace the silver screen. His characters were always worthy of admiration, in spite of their criminal activities. Intelligent men, they were known for their smooth and polished manner and the inimitable Greenstreet chuckle.

As a saloon owner who moonlights in the black market in **Casablanca**, Greenstreet was a 'bad guy,' but he was nevertheless a gentleman. As we discover later in the film, Ferrari feels compelled to offer free advice to the beautiful Ilsa Lund Laszlo and her heroic husband, Victor.

After meeting with Major Strasser, Victor Laszlo goes to the Blue Parrot, hoping to obtain exit visas. While Ilsa waits outside for him (*left*), she meets Rick, who has just left Señor Ferrari.

Rick attempts to apologize for his rude behavior the night before. Maintaining a distance, she finally reveals the truth—that Victor Laszlo is her husband.

After a year at Stockholm's Royal Dramatic Theater School, Ingrid Bergman was on her way to becoming Sweden's hottest young star. Her performance in Gustaf Molander's **Intermezzo** (1936) so mesmerized producer David O Selznick that he brought her to Hollywood to star in the 1939 American version of the same film. The next year found her on Broadway, captivating critics and audiences alike with her performance in *Liliom*.

Returning to Hollywood, she appeared in a few films before her landmark performance in **Casablanca**. From that point on, Bergman appeared in a succession of hits—**For Whom the Bell Tolls** (1943), **Gaslight** (1944), **The Bells of St Mary's** (1945) **Notorious** (1946) and **Joan of Arc** (1948). In the eyes of the American public, she could do no wrong, but she fell from grace when she deserted her husband, Peter Lindstrom, and their daughter, Pia, for Italian director Roberto Rossellini. They married in 1950 amid cries of public outrage.

Scandalized that both Bergman and Rossellini had left their spouses and lived together until they could be married, moviegoers in the United States and other countries boycotted their films.

The marriage proved a disaster for both their careers. The films they did together, of which **Stromboli** (1949) is the best known, were critical and commercial failures. Assailed by religious groups, women's clubs and politicians, Bergman disappeared from the American film world for seven years, her career seemingly over. But in 1956 she was again in the limelight, first, with her performance in Renoir's **Elena et les Hommes/Paris Does Strange Things** and then **Anastasia**, for which she received her second Academy Award (the first was for **Gaslight**).

Even as her career was reviving, her relationship with Rossellini was disintegrating and their marriage was annulled in 1958. She then married Swedish stage producer Lars Schmidt and spent the remainder of her career, some 20 years, appearing in foreign and American films, including **Indiscreet** (1958), **The Inn of the Sixth Happiness** (1958), **Cactus Flower** (1969) and **Autumn Sonata** (1978). She won her third Oscar, for Best Supporting Actress in **Murder on the Orient Express** (1974), and her final performance as Golda Meir in the made-for-TV movie **A Woman Called Golda** (1982) was critically acclaimed.

Previous pages: Ingrid Bergman was not the first choice to play Ilsa Lund Laszlo. Ann Sheridan, Warners' 'Oomph Girl,' had been the original choice; Hedy Lamarr had also been considered, but Metro-Goldwyn-Mayer wouldn't loan her out; and Michele Morgan, a French actress, had been tested. Finally, producer Hal Wallis decided that Ingrid Bergman was his 'first choice, ideal for the foreign girl with a slight accent.' To get Bergman, Wallis had to strike a deal with David O Selznick.

Having acquired the beautiful star, Warner Bros made the most of her beauty in a number of promotional stills. In this still with Sydney Greenstreet, Ingrid's expression reveals Ilsa's trepidation when she learns that Ferrari cannot help her and Laszlo obtain *two* exit visas.

Above: Major Strasser meets with his Nazi henchmen and Renault to discuss Victor Laszlo.

Right: A thoughtful Rick listens to a young woman's (Joy Page) story. She and her husband, Jan, have fled Bulgaria, with the dream of going to America. In spite of his statements to the contrary, Rick does lend his support to those in need. After listening to the young woman's story, Rick allows her husband to win at the roulette table (*overleaf*) so that they can buy their way to freedom.

Left: When Sascha learns that Rick has helped the young couple, he cannot contain his enthusiasm and runs from behind the bar to kiss Rick, telling him, 'Boss, you have done a beautiful thing.'

One of the things that makes **Casablanca** work is that it makes us feel good. In his own emotional, excited way, Sascha has expressed what the audience is feeling. Even though Rick has a reputation for being a hardened individualist, he has—at no small expense—rescued the young Bulgarian couple and thus is behaving as we believe a hero should.

Though there is no profit in it for him, Ferrari tells Laszlo to see Rick about the letters of transit. Laszlo and Ilsa go to Rick's a second night and Laszlo asks to speak to Rick alone (*left*). Citing his past heroic endeavors, Laszlo appeals to Rick's sense of righteousness and asks that he sell him the stolen letters of transit. Rick replies that he prefers not to take sides, that he is 'just a saloon keeper,' but when Laszlo presses him for a reason for his refusal, Rick tells him 'Ask your wife.'

Their conversation interrupted by a rousing chorus of *Die Wacht am Rhein*, the two men rush out of Rick's office (*overleaf*).

Paul Henreid was reluctant to take the part of Victor Laszlo. Already an established leading man, his previous performance in **Now, Voyager** opposite Bette Davis had made him one of Hollywood's hottest stars. Henreid was concerned that the part of Victor was not only a comedown but a foolish role. Henreid himself had fled Vienna when the Nazis marched on the city, and to his mind, hobnobbing with Nazis in a North African nightclub hardly provided a realistic view of life. Warner Bros agreed to build up the part so that he would accept it, and he, in turn, infused the part with an idealistic dignity.

Right: In a demonstration of the mounting political tension in Casablanca, Laszlo leads the crowd in an emotional rendition of *La Marseillaise*, drowning out the German voices singing *Die Wacht am Rhein*. Dismayed by this show of patriotic fervor, Major Strasser orders Captain Renault to close the bar.

The scene is one the film's classic moments, but its filming was far less dramatic. Director Curtiz told Bogey all he had to do for the day was nod his head. Unable to get an explanation from Curtiz as to why he was nodding, Bogart finally gave in and nodded. The famous Bogey nod showed up on film as Rick's signal to the band to follow Victor's lead.

Above: Having triumphed in song, Victor and the French patriots celebrate their symbolic victory by raising their glasses in a toast.

Overleaf: Rick meets with Carl to see how long he can afford to stay closed. Carl starts to tell Rick that he is on his way to the underground meeting, but Rick prefers not to know such things. Victor Laszlo will be at the meeting, too, and before the night is over, he will be back at Rick's Café Américain.

Above: Moments after he walks into Rick's, Victor is greeted by a member of the local resistance movement, who identifies himself by discreetly showing Victor his ring. The face of the ring opens, revealing the symbol of the Fighting French.

Right: The next night Victor makes contact with the underground, but the meeting is raided by the Nazis, and Victor escapes with a bullet wound on the wrist.

Left: After Victor has failed to persuade Rick to sell the letters of transit, Ilsa, in one of the movie's most emotional scenes, goes to Rick. At first, she uses the same tactics that Victor used, speaking of the noble cause for which they are all fighting. When that approach fails, she pulls a gun on him and demands the letters. Rick tells her to 'Go ahead and shoot. You'd be doing me a favor.' Only Bogey could carry off a line like that.

Unable to carry out her threat, Ilsa tells Rick she still loves him, concluding, 'I don't know what's right anymore. You'll have to think for both of us.'

For publicity purposes, studios often used photos that took the actors out of character. In the case of **Casablanca**, however, a scenario such as this *almost* did happen. The script was being finished as the movie was being filmed, and no one knew who would 'get the girl.' Both Bogart and Paul Henreid, who played Victor Laszlo, insisted that he be the one to walk off with Ilsa at the film's conclusion. Elegant and gallant, Henreid was the prototype of the Continental lover and therefore a logical choice.

Then, there was Bogey as Rick. Renault said it best when he told Ilsa, 'He's the kind of man that, well, if I were a woman. . .I should be in love with Rick.' All the audience had to do was look at Ilsa looking at Rick to understand that it made sense for Ilsa to leave with Rick. As a solution to this dilemma director Michael Curtiz considered having Victor die a hero's death. In that way, Henreid's credibility as a leading man would not suffer, while the character of Ilsa would be free to walk off with Rick.

Right: After Ilsa's second visit, Rick goes to see Renault, who reiterates his warning that Rick not assist Laszlo's escape. Rick responds by telling Louis that he plans to leave Casablanca with Ilsa, and to ensure that this plan works, he wants Louis to arrive at Rick's just as he is handing the letters of transit over to Laszlo, thereby giving the Prefect of Police the grounds he needs to arrest Laszlo... or so he says.

As the film races to a climax, Victor and Ilsa arrive at Rick's. The next few moments will be filled with surprises for everyone except Rick, who has carefully engineered the moment.

The narrative pace of the film, which has moved quickly up to this point, now moves at an even faster pace. Although director Curtiz reportedly said that he *had* to keep the film moving at breakneck speed in order to conceal the holes in the plot, **Casablanca** can hardly be dismissed as 'the happiest of happy accidents,' to quote critic Andrew Sarris. Indeed, **Casablanca**, which won Curtiz an Academy Award, is one of the finest films that he did for Warner Bros.

Curtiz worked in every film genre imaginable—social dramas, musical comedies, Westerns, swashbucklers, prison and gangster melodramas, horror films, and thrillers. The films he did with Errol Flynn—including **Captain Blood** (1935), **The Charge of the Light Brigade** (1936), **The Adventures of Robin Hood** (1938), and **The Sea Hawk** (1940)—rank among Hollywood's best romantic adventures. In addition to **Casablanca**, Curtiz worked with Bogart in several other films, including **Angels With Dirty Faces** (1938), and made several notable films with John Garfield and James Cagney. He resurrected Joan Crawford's career with **Mildred Pierce** (1945).

Known as a dictator on the set, Curtiz ruled his actors and technicians with an iron hand—and was hated by both. After he left Warner Bros in the 1950s, the quality of his films deteriorated, which had the unfortunate effect of diminishing his earlier achievements.

Left: Renault tells Victor he is under arrest as an accessory to the murder of the German couriers, and as he explains Rick's part in the drama, ('It seems love has triumphed over virtue') Renault will soon be in for his own surprise...

By this point in the film, first-time viewers are practically jumping out of their seats, wondering what will happen next. Even those who have seen **Casablanca** a dozen times are caught up in the excitement.

Its fans consider **Casablanca** the best Hollywood movie of all time, and the film was justly rewarded at the sixteenth annual Academy Awards in 1943. In all, **Casablanca** was nominated for eight Academy Awards. Humphrey Bogart was nominated for Best Actor, Claude Rains for Best Supporting Actor, Arthur Edeson for Best Cinematography (B & W), Owen Marks for Best Film Editing and Max Steiner for Best Musical Score. Michael Curtiz walked away with an Oscar for Best Director, Julius Epstein, Philip Epstein and Howard Koch won for Best Screenplay and **Casablanca** won Best Picture.

Right: Rick turns his gun on Louis, but Louis has a few tricks of his own. Instead of calling the airport to ensure that Victor and Ilsa can leave unhindered, he alerts Major Strasser to their planned departure.

Soon all the tangled story threads will be woven neatly into place. Although the script was not completed until the final hour, the conclusion turned out to be one of the finest, most satisfying in film history. The finished product earned screenwriters Julius and Philip Epstein and Howard Koch an Academy Award for Best Screenplay.

Julius Epstein began his career as a radio publicist before turning to writing one-act plays and then screenplays. In 1939, he began a successful collaboration of nearly 20 years with his brother, Philip. The pair collaborated on a number of films during Warner Bros' heyday.

Howard Koch graduated from Columbia with a law degree, but soon established a career as a writer rather than as an attorney. He began writing plays and then radio scripts, most notably **War of the Worlds**. In 1940, he turned to Hollywood and over the next decade established an excellent reputation for himself. In 1951, however, Hollywood yielded to pressure from the House of Un-American Activities Committee and placed Koch on its notorious blacklist. Koch eventually moved to England, finally returning to screenwriting in the early 1960s.

Previous pages: Renault, Rick, Victor and Ilsa arrive at the airport.

Left: One of the most unforgettable scenes ever to come out of Hollywood is that of Ilsa and Rick, shrouded in fog, as they bid each other farewell. Standing in his trench coat and fedora, Rick looks into Ilsa's tear-filled eyes and tells her, 'Look, I'm no good at being noble, but it doesn't take much to see that the problems of three little people don't amount to a hill of beans in this crazy world. Someday you'll understand that.'

Overleaf: Only moments after Ilsa and Victor have boarded their plane, Major Strasser arrives. When he attempts to stop the plane, Rick shoots him, but Renault is on his side and gives the order to 'Round up the usual suspects.' In a conclusion guaranteed to encourage cheers from the audience, Rick and Louis walk off in the fog together, united in purpose.

INDEX

Academy Awards 6, 35, 48, 75, 103
African Queen, The 35
Alison, Joan 29
Angels With Dirty Faces 101
As Time Goes By 11, 36, 42, 51

Bacall, Lauren 35, 52
Barefoot Contessa, The 35, 42
Bells of St Mary's, The 45, 75
Bergman, Ingrid 1, 2, 6, 8, 9, 10, 11, 36, 37-39, 43, 44, 45, 48-49, 50-53, 56-57, 60, 60, 63, 68-69, 74, 75, 76-77, 78, 92, 94, 102, 104-109, 112
Big Sleep, The 35
Bogart, Humphrey 2, 6, 7, 8, 9, 16-17, 17, 18-19, 19, 21-23, 26-27, 34-35, 35, 38-41, 43, 44, 46, 48-51, 52, 53, 54, 56-59, 60, 60-61, 70-73, 78-79, 82-84, 88, 90-91, 94, 95, 96, 97, 102, 103, 104-112
British Film Institute 6
Burnett, Murray 29

Caine Mutiny, The 35
Churchill, Winston 66
Curtiz, Michael 6, 8, 9, 11, 32, 60, 60-63, 63, 97, 98, 101, 103

Davis, Bette 8, 85
de Gaulle, General Charles 12, 64

Edeson, Arthur 45, 103
Eisenhower, General Dwight D 66
Epstein, Julius 11, 103-104
Epstein, Philip 11, 103-104
Everybody Comes to Rick's 29

Gaslight 75
Gone With the Wind 48, 52
Greenstreet, Sydney 11, 20, 20-23, 72-73, 73, 76-77, 78

Henreid, Paul 1, 2, 8, 38-39, 63, 68-69, 84, 85, 86-89, 92-93, 97, 102, 104-107, 112
Hitler, Adolf 64

Intermezzo 8, 75

Joan of Arc 45, 75

Key Largo 35
Kinskey, Leonid 14-15, 15, 82-83
Koch, Howard 11, 103-104

Lamarr, Hedy 78
LeBeau, Madeline 24-25, 25
Lorre, Peter 11, 16-17, 17, 32-35
Lukas, Paul 23

M 17
Maltese Falcon, The 8, 17, 20, 54, 63
Marks, Owen 103
Mask of Dimitrios, The 17, 47

Morgan, Michele 78

Now, Voyager 8, 48, 85

Page, Joy 78, 78-79
Pétain, Marshal Henri 64
Petrified Forest, The 54

Rains, Claude 1, 11, 13, 26-29, 29, 30-31, 64, 64-65, 66, 67, 68, 78, 98-99, 102, 103, 104-107, 110
Reagan, Ronald 6
Roosevelt, Franklin Delano 66

Sakall, SZ 11, 14-15, 15, 82-83, 90-91
Selznick, David O 8, 78
Sheridan, Ann 6, 75
Steiner, Max 6, 11, 48, 103

Three Strangers 17, 45
To Have and Have Not 35, 52
TV Guide 6

Veidt, Conrad 13, 29, 30, 30-31, 64, 64-65, 66, 67, 69, 78, 110
Verdict, The 17
Vichy 12, 64

Wallis, Hal B 63, 78
Warner Bros 11, 20, 54, 78, 85, 98

Wilson, Dooley 6, 11, 18-19, 19, 46, 47, 50-51, 63
Woollcott, Alexander 54

Left: The stars of **Casablanca**—Claude Rains, Paul Henreid, Ingrid Bergman and Humphrey Bogart.

Page 112: Paul Henreid, Ingrid Bergman and Humphrey Bogart—the stars of one of Hollywood's finest movies—gather in front of Rick's Café Américain, the most famous saloon in the world.
Here's looking at you, kids.